Mankind: Anthropolc  *y*

CONTENTS

Alpha Omega Publications®

804 N. 2nd Ave. E., Rock Rapids, IA 51246-1759

© MCMXCVIII by Alpha Omega Publications, Inc. All rights reserved.

LIFEPAC is a registered trademark of Alpha Omega Publications, Inc.

Dear Instructor,

Thank you for your interest in electives using the LIFEPAC Select Series.

The courses in this series have been compiled by schools using Alpha Omega's LIFEPAC Curriculum. These courses are an excellent example of the flexibility of the LIFEPAC Curriculum for specialized teaching purposes.

The unique design of the worktext format has allowed instructors to mix and match LIFEPACs from five core subjects (Bible, History & Geography, Language Arts, Math, and Science) to create alternative courses for junior high and high school credit.

These courses work particularly well as unit studies, as supplementary electives, or for meeting various school and state requirements. Another benefit of the courses—and any LIFEPAC subject, for that matter—is the ability to use them with any curriculum, at any time during the year, for any of several purposes:

- Elective Courses
- Make-up Courses
- Substitution Courses
- Unit Studies

- Summer School Courses
- Remedial Courses
- Multi-level Teaching
- Thematic Studies

Course Titles	*Suggested Credits*
Astronomy (Jr. High and above)	$\frac{1}{2}$ credit
Composition	$\frac{1}{2}$ credit
Geography	$\frac{1}{2}$ credit
Geology	$\frac{1}{2}$ credit
Life of Christ (Jr. High and above)	$\frac{1}{2}$ credit
Life Science	$\frac{1}{2}$ credit
Mankind: Anthropology and Sociology	$\frac{1}{2}$ credit

Mankind: Anthropology & Sociology

High School Level (1/2 credit)

Mankind
Bible LIFEPAC 702

The Origin of Mankind
- The Creation of Man
- The Original Nature of Man

The Fall of Mankind
- The Reasons for Man's Fall
- The Results of Man's Fall

The Re-creation of Man
- The Method of Re-creation
- The Results of Re-creation

The Mission of Man
- God's Original Mission
- God's Renewed Mission

Anthropology
History & Geography
LIFEPAC 704

The Study of Man
- The Basis of Anthropology
- The Science of Anthropology

The Nature of Man
- The Unity of Man
- The Diversity of Man

The Culture of Man
- Seeking Food
- Seeking Protection
- Seeking Prosperity

Sociology–Man in Groups
History & Geography
LIFEPAC 705

An Introduction to Sociology
- Definition
- Relationship to Other Subjects
- Historical Development
- Major Interests
- Importance to Christians

The Method of Sociology
- Theory
- Description
- Statistics
- Surveys
- Experimentation
- Field Observation

Anthropology and Sociology of the United States
History & Geography
LIFEPAC 706

Cultural Backgrounds of the United States
- Native Americans
- Other Cultural Groups

Sociology and Culture of Groups from Distant Lands
- Immigrants from Europe, Asia, and Africa
- Other Social Groups
- Religions of the Groups

Cultural and Social Interaction
- United States as a Melting Pot
- Change in Society

The Earth and Man
History & Geography
LIFEPAC 906

The Earth Is Man's Home
- Man Inhabits the Earth
- Man Survives the Flood
- Man Covers the Earth
- Man Begins History

The Earth Is Developed by Man
- Development of Civilizations
- Development of Resources
- Development of Water Transport Systems
- Development of Cities

The Earth Has a Future
- World Leaders Pursue Peace
- Divine Judgment Brings Peace

Materials Needed for LIFEPAC

Required:

Suggested:
Bible dictionary
Bible concordance
thesaurus
Bible, King James Version or other
   versions if permitted

Additional Learning Activities

Section I – The Origin of Mankind

1. In what way was man made in the image of God?
2. Why did God give man the freedom to choose between good and evil, knowing that this freedom could lead to spiritual and physical death?
3. God is your friend. Write a letter to Him as you would to your best friend sharing some of your disappointments, joys, and hopes for the future.
4. A thinking question: If everything God created was "good," do we have a right to criticize ourselves and to run ourselves down needlessly? Is this criticizing one of God's creations?

Section II – The Fall of Mankind

1. Do you think it's fair that because Adam sinned, we are born with sin in our hearts? Should we be held responsible for his sin? (We are not held responsible for his sin; we will only be judged by the sins we have committed. However, we are born with a sinful nature and have a choice between good and evil.)
2. Write and produce a conversation between Satan and Eve, Eve and Adam, and among God, Adam, and Eve after Adam and Eve had sinned.
3. Students should make a class newspaper covering the Creation to the Fall. The paper may include items on what was created on each day. Other articles could describe Adam and Eve, God's fellowship with Adam and Eve, the serpent, the temptation, the sin, and Adam and Eve's expulsion from the garden.
4. Think of at least five other Bible characters who yielded to Satan's temptations. Write their names and a brief description of the sin. (Saul, David, Abraham, Judas, Ananias and Sapphira, etc.)

Section III – The Re-Creation of Man

1. Christ promises that if we receive Him, we will have abundant life on earth and eternal life after death. If there was not a heaven after death, if death was the end, would you still serve Christ for the abundant life He gives you on earth?
2. The Bible tells us that man "looketh on the outward appearance, but God looketh on the heart," and "Judge not, that ye be not judged." It also says, "Ye shall know them by their fruits." Do you think you can tell by watching and listening to a person whether or not he is a Christian? (Bring out the idea that things are not always what they seem, and that we do not know the motive behind a person's actions.)

Point out also that people are watching us, and although we live to please God and not people, we still have to be careful of our words and actions so we will not bring reproach to God's name.

3. Let the class have a contest to see who can get the most words out of "re-creation." No letters can be repeated unless more than one of that letter appears in the word. Share the list with the class.

4. Pair off by two's (or in small groups). Select one or two in each group to explain to the others why we are born with sin and how we can be forgiven of those sins and become Christians. Others in the group may ask questions or help answer questions.

5. Make a list of ways you believe God's love differs from man's love.

6. Thinking question: If we have everything we want materially, can we still be happy without Christ? Find Scripture to back up your answer.

Section IV – The Mission of Man

1. Genesis 3:16 says the husband shall rule over the wife. Do you think this command is a result of the Fall? (Point out the Bible commandment that the man is the head of the house.)

2. Can we be Christians without anyone knowing it? (Point out that part of our responsibility as Christians is to share Christ with others.)

3. Using ideas from the class, write a song or choral arrangement telling the story of the Creation, the Fall, and salvation. (A music teacher might help with this activity.) If this activity is too difficult, perhaps a story-poem could be composed.

4. Discuss the question, "If God forgives us our sin, why do we find it hard to forgive ourselves?" Discuss the phrase, "healing of the memories." Have a spokesman report to the class.

5. Have students share with the class how their lives have been changed since Jesus came into their hearts. Try to give something specific.

6. Make a list of how this world would be different today if Christ had not come.

7. Think of one friend of yours who needs the Lord. Pray for a chance to witness to that friend this week. Ask the Lord to show you Scripture verses to help in your witness. Include your own personal testimony of how your life has been different since Christ came into your heart.

SECTION ONE

1.1 Genesis

1.2 creation

1.3 body

1.4 evolve

1.5 dust

1.6 c

1.7 a

1.8 b

1.9 Example: God made him from the dust of the earth and breathed into his nostrils the breath of life, and man became a living soul.

1.10 Example: To make something, you start with something and build upon it. To create, you make something from nothing.

1.11 Examples; any order:
   a. created in God's image
   b. had fellowship with God
   c. lived in the Garden of Eden
   d. had a personal choice to obey or disobey God

1.12 The Bible says God pronounced His creation very good.

1.13 Examples; any order:
   a. was naked and unashamed
   b. no evil in him
   c. had perfect fellowship with God

1.14 Image means a likeness of or similarity to something else.

1.15

   ACROSS
   2. God
   3. Adam
   5. garden
   7. image
   8. sin

   DOWN
   1. woman
   4. animals
   6. death

1.16 a. create   b. ed
   c. enjoy   d. ed
   e. like   f. ness
   g. absolute   h. ly

1.17 a. to do something of one's own free will
   b. friendship; to walk and talk together; sharing together
   c. without shame

1.18 Examples:
   a. mankind
   b. understand
   Examples:
   c. Mankind was God's highest creation.
   d. Did you understand the question?

SECTION TWO

2.1	devil		2.17	b
2.2	heaven		2.18	h
2.3	dethrone		2.19	e
2.4	third		2.20	i

2.5   earth

2.6   tempter

2.7   serpent

2.8   dethrone

2.9   death

2.10   disobey

2.11   j

2.12   g

2.13   c

2.14   f

2.15   a

2.16   d

2.21   Example: Adam disobeyed God's law and ate of the fruit of the tree of knowledge after God told him not to.

2.22   Example: Adam was tempted to distrust God as an honest and loving God.

2.23   Example: Adam and Eve suffered physical death, separation from God, and physical suffering.

2.24   Example: Because of the sin of Adam and Eve, all human nature is separated from God. People need redemption through Jesus Christ.

SECTION THREE

3.1   Love is God's motive for redeeming mankind.

3.2   God sent Jesus, His only son, to die upon the cross as penalty for mankind's sins.

3.3   Death passed upon all men.

3.4   The lamb sacrifice showed that soon a perfect sacrifice, Jesus, would be offered once and for all mankind.

3.5   Spiritual fellowship with God is restored when a person accepts Jesus as personal Savior.

3.6   a.   dethrone

b.   confronted

c.   disobedience

d.   re-creation

e.   Redemption

f.   resurrection

3.7

	in bondage to sin	free from sin
a.	in bondage to sin	free from sin
b.	loss of fellowship with God	restored fellowship with God
c.	servant of the the devil	servant of the Lord

3.8   Adult check

3.9

ACROSS

1. dethrone
5. Genesis
6. evolve
7. origin
8. eternal
9. despair

DOWN

1. disobedience
2. tempter
3. redemption
4. nature
10. administered

SECTION FOUR

4.1 Example: Man was placed in the Garden of Eden after he was created.

4.2 Adam's mission was to tend the Garden of Eden.

4.3 In any order:
   a. to keep the garden: to dress it, and to enjoy the fruit of his labor;
   b. to be fruitful: to multiply, and to replenish the earth;
   c. to subdue the earth: to have dominion over it;
   d. to enjoy all of God creation: all the earth was at peace; and
   e. to fellowship with God: to walk and talk with Him; to enjoy His company

4.4 Example: She ate of the fruit of the tree of the knowledge of good and evil, disobeying God.

4.5 Any three; any order:
   a. Their sorrow would be multiplied
   b. Man would rule over woman
   c. Man would labor for his bread
   d. Man would return to dust (die)
   e. They were driven from the garden.

4.6 Today we are under the same bondage that began at the time of creation and man's fall through sin.

4.7 receive Jesus Christ as his personal Savior

4.8 God once again finds pleasure in our lives, and we become children of God. We are again restored into a position of authority and peace.

4.9 His pleasure

4.10 Any order:
   a. We are once again restored into a position of authority and peace.
   b. We are new creatures.
   c. We become children of God.

4.11 Either order:
   a. mind
   b. spirit

4.12 a. remission
   b. nations

4.13 We have all sinned and come short of God's glory

4.14 Example: We are all sinners by birth and have lost the pleasure of God. It also tells us that God isn't pleased with sin and will punish us by not allowing us entrance into heaven.

4.15 disobedience

4.16 Any two:
   a. sorrow (trouble)
   b. God's displeasure
   or spiritual and physical death expelled from Eden

4.17 For the wages of sin is death; but the gift of God is eternal life through Jesus Christ our Lord.

4.18 Example: Those who trust Jesus Christ as personal Savior are no longer under God's condemnation or judgement.

SELF TEST 1

1.01	o	1.021	a
1.02	f	1.022	a, b
1.03	a	1.023	the end of one's life on earth
1.04	g	1.024	man's moral and emotional nature
1.05	b	1.025	to do something of one's own free will
1.06	c	1.026	to bring into existence from nothing
1.07	m	1.027	likeness
1.08	d	1.028	beginning
1.09	e	1.029	Any two of these:
1.010	n		a. could have fellowship with God
1.011	h		b. could choose right or wrong
1.012	k		c. was a living soul
1.013	i		d. had a spirit and body
1.014	j	1.030	God created man from the dust of the
1.015	l		earth. God's creation of man was a spe-
1.016	knowledge		cial act of God. Man had a body, but man
1.017	man		also became a "living soul" when God
1.018	law		breathed into him the breath of life.
1.019	chose		
1.020	death		

SELF TEST 2

2.01	b	2.020	confronted
2.02	b	2.021	created
2.03	b	2.022	nature
2.04	c	2.023	Genesis
2.05	c	2.024	image
2.06	death	2.025	Because of the sin of Adam and Eve, peo-
2.07	In any order:		ple are born with sinful natures and are
	a. body		separated from God. The people must be
	b. spirit		saved through God's redemption plan.
	c. soul	2.026	God created Adam from the dust of the
2.08	sin		earth. God breathed into Adam's nostrils
2.09	confronted		the breath of life. Adam became a living
2.010	paying a price to buy back		soul.
2.011	an act of disobedience against God	2.027	Because of Adam's disobedience, the
2.012	made from nothing		curse of sin was placed upon all
2.013	emotional and moral nature of man		mankind. Therefore, if we are to be with
2.014.	to replace one's rule with another		Jesus in heaven, we must accept Him as
2.015	d		our personal Savior.
2.016	e	2.028	God put the tree of knowledge in the gar-
2.017	a		den to give man a choice to either obey or
2.018	b		disobey God.
2.019	c		

SELF TEST 3

3.01	e
3.02	m
3.03	c
3.04	i
3.05	h
3.06	g
3.07	j
3.08	k
3.09	l
3.010	n
3.011	o
3.012	f
3.013	b
3.014	d
3.015	a
3.016	false
3.017	true
3.018	false
3.019	true
3.020	false
3.021	true

3.022 false
3.023 true
3.024 true
3.025 true
3.026 death
3.027 a. life
     b. abundantly
3.028 eternal
3.029 Salvation
3.030 Either order:
     a. eternal life
     b. abundant life
3.031 free
3.032 soul
3.033 love
3.034 separated
3.035 Example: Death passed upon all of us. Therefore, we are all separated from God and need to accept the finished work of Jesus for our personal salvation.

SELF TEST 4

4.01	d
4.02	j
4.03	g
4.04	a
4.05	i
4.06	e
4.07	h
4.08	k
4.09	c
4.010	b

4.011 Either order:
     a. mind
     b. spirit
4.012 Confronted
4.013 death
4.014 love
4.015 Any order:
     a. to have dominion over the earth
     b. to care for the garden
     c. to multiply and replenish the earth
     d. to enjoy divine fellowship

4.016 In any order:
     a. fellowship with God was broken – separation from God
     b. physical suffering
     c. physical death
4.017 false
4.018 true
4.019 false
4.020 true
4.021 true
4.022 false
4.023 true
4.024 true
4.025 1
4.026 3
4.027 6:5
4.028 6:23
4.029 Example: Man's only hope today is salvation through a personal faith in Jesus Christ.

Bible 702
LIFEPAC Test

1.	f	26.	2
2.	g	27.	4
3.	h	28.	6
4.	j	29.	3
5.	b	30.	1
6.	e	31.	5
7.	i		

32. After their sin, human nature was separated from God. People would need to be saved through the blood of Jesus and to accept Him as Savior.

8. c

9. d

10. a

11. true

12. true

13. true

14. true

15. false

16. true

17. true

18. true

19. false

20. true

21. earth

22. image

23. just

24. spirit

25. dominion

Bible 702 Alternate Test

Name _____

Match these items (Each answer, 2 points).

1. _____ never ending
2. _____ disobey God's law
3. _____ penalty of sin
4. _____ create from nothing
5. _____ material from which Adam was created
6. _____ to have authority
7. _____ test
8. _____ disposition of a person
9. _____ to greatly desire
10. _____ the beginning

a. create
b. eternal
c. dominion
d. tempt
e. sin
f. nature
g. crave
h. Genesis
i. dust
j. death
k. evil

Answer *true* or *false* (each answer, 1 point).

11. _____ Adam voluntarily sinned against God's law.
12. _____ The tempter was already cast out of heaven before the fall of man.
13. _____ Spiritual death is separation from God's presence.
14. _____ Old Testament sacrifice was a symbol pointing to the death of Christ.
15. _____ Salvation is based upon merit or personal works.
16. _____ The word *origin* means *evolution*.
17. _____ Adam could eat of the tree of life.
18. _____ Satan is also called the Tempter.
19. _____ Re-creation involves change.
20. _____ Some people were born saved.

Complete these statements (each answer, 3 points).

21. Jesus came that we might have a. _____ and have it

more b. _____ .

22. The trick the devil used on the woman was to question God's _____ .

23. Adam's sin was _____ to God's law.

24. The reason we need salvation is because _____ has passed upon all men.

25. God first created man's a. _____ and then created his

b. _____ .

26. The account of Creation is found in the book of _____ .

27. Adam and Eve's first two sons were named a. _____ and

    b. _____ .

28. The devil _____ Adam and the woman.

29. God is just and cannot overlook _____ .

30. We should share the _____ about Christ with others.

Write the letter for the correct answer on each line (each answer, 2 points).

31. The method God used to begin the human race was _____ .
    a. evolution   c. creation
    b. building   d. a, b, and c

32. God made man in His own _____ .
    a. will   c. image
    b. time   d. love

33. The act of buying back is called _____ .
    a. confronted   c. redemption
    b. transaction   d. salvation

34. The motive behind God's making salvation available is _____ .
    a. wrath   c. righteousness
    b. envy   d. love

35. God created man with a free _____ .
    a. nature   c. will
    b. image   d. none of these

Answer these questions (each answer, 5 points).

36. Why does every person need to receive Jesus Christ as their Savior?

    _____

    _____

    _____

37. What are the benefits of salvation? _____

    _____

    _____

38. How can a person be saved? _____

    _____

    _____

    _____

75 / 94

Date _____

Score _____

1. b
2. e
3. j
4. a
5. i
6. c
7. d
8. f
9. g
10. h
11. true
12. true
13. true
14. true
15. false
16. false
17. true
18. true
19. true
20. false
21. a. life
    b. abundantly
22. word
23. disobedience
24. death
25. a. body
    b. spirit
26. Genesis
27. Either order:
    a. Cain
    b. Abel
28. tempted
29. sin
30. good news
31. c
32. c
33. c
34. d
35. c
36. Hint: answers should include the idea that all are sinners
37. eternal life and abundant life
38. in prayer, receive Jesus Christ as Lord and Savior

Materials Needed for LIFEPAC

Required: Suggested:
None   encyclopedia
                                       atlas

Additional Learning Activities

Section I The Study of Man

1. Discuss the differences between anthropologists and other scientists, such as biologists, astronomers, physicists, and so forth. What do anthropologists do that no other scientists do?

2. Have students keep a diary of a week in their school life as if they were fieldworkers from another society. Have them read portions of their diaries aloud.

3. Ask a friend to read about and discuss a foreign society in which he may be interested. At the end of his presentation point out to him areas in which he seemed to be showing bias or prejudice.

4. Discuss with friends the major features of American culture today. Of what features do you think God approves? Of which features do you think he disapproves?

5. Obtain a new or used copy of *National Geographic* magazine. Find in it a story about a culture that is completely different from our own. What methods do you think the author used to learn what he did? Would you enjoy being a member of that culture?

6. If an archaeologist a thousand years from now goes through the remains of your house, what will he find? What will it tell him about you? If you left a note behind for him to read so he could understand you better, what would the note say?

7. Write a one-page report on the discovery of the tomb of King Tutankhamen by an archaeologist.

Section II The Nature of Man

1. Discuss ways in which all people everywhere are the same. Are people all alike physically? Do all people have a religion? A language? A government?

2. How does the Bible tell us the races were formed? What are the names given to the three race divisions? Who started them?

3. Discuss with a friend how people around the world are different from one another. Does this difference lead to wars? If not, what does?

4. Write a short paper describing how you would deal with a stranger from another land. He is totally different in appearance from you, he dresses differently from anyone you have ever seen, and he speaks no English. Nevertheless, he wants to be friends. What would you do?

5. Make a bulletin board of pictures illustrating the differences between peoples.

Section III The Culture of Man

1. Invite an anthropologist or a missionary to visit the class.
2. How has man affected his environment? Has the effect been all good, all bad, or some of each?
3. What is a potlatch? Hold an imaginary potlatch among your friends, giving away your valuable possessions one by one until they are gone. Do you see any reason for such a ceremony? Why, or why not?
4. Plan some meals you would have if you lived in a strictly horticultural society. Exchange meal plans and look over each other's. Would you enjoy this kind of diet?
5. Read the entry about "anthropology" in your encyclopedia, and write a brief summary of it.
6. Describe how the "rites of passage" are conducted in the United States.

SECTION ONE

1.1 **ACROSS**
    1. generalization
    2. haphazard
    3. contemporary
    4. comprehensive
    5. band
    6. ethnographer
  DOWN
    1. genealogical
    2. ethics
    3. etiquette
    4. bias
    5. divination
    6. folklore

1.2 "the science of man"

1.3 ethnologists

1.4 past

1.5 physical anthropologists

1.6 archaeologists

1.7 c

1.8 e

1.9 g

1.10 i

1.11 k

1.12 a

1.13 j

1.14 h

1.15 f

1.16 d

1.17 b

1.18 Either order:
    a. ancient
    b. modern

1.19 The nonliterate peoples were dying out. Passing ways of life need to be recorded.

1.20 c

1.21 b

1.22 d

1.23 d

1.24 The goal of anthropology is to discover the similarities in human custom between groups.

1.25 He discovered that birth, puberty, marriage, and death are always accompanied by ceremonies.

1.26 a. birth

1.27 b. puberty

1.28 c. marriage

1.29 d. death

1.30 a. birth

1.31 b. puberty

1.32 d. death

1.33 c. marriage

1.34 Any order:
    a. trade
    b. games
    c. tool making
    d. personal names
    e. music

1.35 The comparative method in anthropology compares similarities and differences among societies.

1.36 regularities
    world-wide
    culture

1.37 The following items should be checked:
    Evaluate culture from native person's point of view.
    Live among the people and participate in their culture.

1.38 d

1.39 f

1.40 g

1.41 a

1.42 e

1.43 b

1.44 false

1.45 true

1.46 false

1.47 false

1.48 true

1.49 participant observation

1.50 key informants

1.51 a. psychological
    b. life

1.52 genealogical

1.53 census

1.54 b

1.55 c

1.56 a

1.57	c		1.61	c
1.58	a		1.62	b
1.59	d		1.63	c
1.60	a		1.64	b

SECTION TWO

2.1 f

2.2 d

2.3 b

2.4 a

2.5 c

2.6 e

2.7 g

2.8 Eve

2.9 a. God
     b. created
     c. image

2.10 dust

2.11 206

2.12 man (Adam)

2.13 **ACROSS**
      1. heterozygous
      2. allele
      3. gene pool
      DOWN
      1. homozygous
      2. taxa
      3. genus

2.14 God

2.15 rule

2.16 shadow

2.17 a. conscious
      b. responsibility

2.18 true

2.19 false

2.20 true

2.21 true

2.22 Either order:
      a. sin
      b. death

2.23 everlasting

2.24 homo
      sapiens

2.25 blood

2.26 fertile

2.27 d

2.28 f

2.29 g

2.30 c

2.31 b

2.32 They received similar genetic material from their parents.

2.33 a. interaction between a pair of alleles
      b. interaction with their environment

2.34 combinations of

2.35 Any order:
      a. population
      b. environment
      c. common language

2.36 language

2.37 barrier

2.38 intramarriage

SECTION THREE

3.1 **ACROSS**
     1. deplete
     2. alliance
     3. lifestyle
     4. intermarriage
     DOWN
     1. durable
     2. clan

     3. alkaloid
     4. inherent

3.2 b

3.3 d

3.4 f

3.5 h

3.6 j

3.7 i

3.8   g

3.9   e

3.10   c

3.11   a

3.12   cultural

3.13   Either order:
     a. hunting
     b. gathering

3.14   move

3.15   dry

3.16   possessions

3.17   Either order:
     a. horticulture
     b. hunting

3.18   protection

3.19   move

3.20   a. Hopi
     b. wind-blown

3.21   rain

3.22   true

3.23   false

3.24   false

3.25   true

3.26   true

3.27   b

3.28   The following items must be checked:
     food
     fuel
     grooming supplies
     wall plaster

3.29   a. dry
     b. rains
     c. scattered

3.30   Any of the following:
It is made from local materials. It protects against the wind and cold. It lasts the whole season.

3.31   Any of the following:
It gives protection from the sun and wind. It gives protection from the cold. It can be built quickly.

3.32   b, c

3.33   a, d

3.34   a, d

3.35   d

3.36   kin

3.37   intermarriage

3.38   kinship

3.39   a. weaker
     b. stronger

3.40   battles

3.41   Example:
To have success in life; to have supernatural ability.

3.42   through visions

3.43   Example:
Some came unsought; through a form of ordeal.

3.44   Example:
By singing a certain song; by wearing something special on his head.

3.45   Magic

3.46   The Indian's method provided nutriments used by the corn; the Zande's method provided nothing the corn could use.

3.47   Both are relying on a supernatural force to grow a good crop.

3.48   arrow

3.49   b

3.50   c

3.51   d

3.52   a

3.53   d

3.54   teacher check
Hint:
Read Deuteronomy 18:10-12; I Samuel 15:23; Proverbs 16:33; Joshua 7:13; Numbers 26:55; I Samuel 10:20; Acts 1:26
Example:
God forbids the use of divination. Its use is an abomination unto the Lord.

SELF TEST 1

1.01   c

1.02   e

1.03   g

1.04   i

1.05   k

1.06   m

1.07   a

1.08   o

1.09   n

1.010   l

1.011   j

1.012   h

1.013   f

1.014   d

1.015   b

1.016   b

1.017   d

1.018   c

1.019   a

1.020   b

1.021   b

1.022   d

1.023   a

1.024   4

1.025   3

1.026   8

1.027   6

1.028   1

1.029   5

1.030   10

1.031   7

1.032   2

1.033   9

1.034   language

1.035   comparative

1.036   Either order:
- a. ethnocentrism
- b. noble savage

1.037   Either order:
- a. kinship chart
- b. census

1.038   culture shock

1.039   participant

1.040   The following items should be checked:
greetings
feasting
law
family
property rights
ethics

SELF TEST 2

2.01   c

2.02   e

2.03   g

2.04   i

2.05   k

2.06   m

2.07   o

2.08   a

2.09   n

2.010   l

2.011   j

2.012   h

2.013   f

2.014   d

2.015   b

2.016   comparative

2.017   Any order:
- a. Mongolid
- b. Negrid
- c. Europid

2.018   dust

2.019   participant observation

2.020   Any order:
- a. population
- b. environment
- c. language

2.021   everlasting

2.022   a. conscious
       b. responsibility

2.023 Any three:
    a. death
    b. birth
    c. puberty
       or marriage
2.024 God
2.025 6
2.026 5
2.027 1

2.028 7
2.029 3
2.030 2
2.031 4
2.032 b
2.033 c
2.034 b
2.035 a

SELF TEST 3

3.01   b
3.02   d
3.03   f
3.04   h
3.05   j
3.06   l
3.07   a
3.08   n
3.09   o
3.010 m
3.011 k
3.012 i
3.013 g
3.014 e
3.015 c
3.016 d
3.017 b
3.018 c
3.019 d
3.020 b
3.021 a
3.022 c
3.023 b

3.024 a
3.025 a
3.026 d
3.027 b
3.028 subdue
3.029 Homo sapiens
3.030 language
3.031 marriage
3.032 Pastoral
3.033 divination
3.034 Any three:
    a. death
    b. birth
    c. puberty
       or marriage
3.035 a. environment
    b. language
3.036 true
3.037 true
3.038 false
3.039 false
3.040 false
3.041 true

History & Geography 704
LIFEPAC Test

1.	b	23.	d	
2.	d	24.	b	
3.	f	25.	a	
4.	h	26.	a	
5.	j	27.	7	
6.	i	28.	2	
7.	g	29.	4	
8.	e	30.	6	
9.	c	31.	5	
10.	a	32.	1	
11.	c	33.	3	
12.	c	34.	a, d	
13.	d	35.	b, c	
14.	b	36.	a, d	
15.	c	37.	c	
16.	e	38.	a, d	
17.	g	39.	a, d	
18.	i	40.	regularities	
19.	a	41.	comparative	
20.	j	42.	participant observation	
21.	h	43.	monograph	
22.	f			

Name _____

Write the letter for the correct answer on the line (each answer, 2 points).

1. Anthropology is the study of _____ .
   a. animals   c. man
   b. birds   d. religion

2. Culture is the way man _____ his environment.
   a. submits   c. submerges
   b. subdues   d. substitutes

3. The cultural regularity discovered by Arnold van Gennep was _____ .
   a. rites of passage   c. kin-groups
   b. folklore   d. tool-making

4. Seeing foreign cultures as inferior to one's own is known as _____ .
   a. game   c. nonliterate
   b. superiority   d. ethnocentrism

5. *Culture shock* is a form of _____ .
   a. violence   c. trauma
   b. anthropology   d. travel

6. The principal task of the fieldworker in anthropology is to gather _____ .
   a. tribes   c. information
   b. kinships   d. berries

7. The type of anthropologist who goes out to study living tribes is known as a(n) _____ .
   a. ethnographer   c. sage
   b. archaeologist   d. sociologist

8. Man is classed by scientists as belonging to the genus *Homo* and species _____ .
   a. pithecanthropus c. human
   b. sapiens   d. taxus

9. The number of bones in the human body is _____ .
   a. 206   c. 12
   b. 52   d. 100

10. To anthropologists, human groups are like _____ .
    a. tools   c. societies
    b. cultures   d. laboratories

Answer *true* or *false* (each answer, 1 point).

11. _____ Anthropology courses are not important for doing fieldwork.
12. _____ An anthropologist knows nothing about a group of people before he goes to live among them.
13. _____ Anthropologists often have difficulty adjusting to a new way of life.
14. _____ Words are sounds that have a specific meaning.
15. _____ Mankind has never had a common language.

16. _____ Clear communication helps a society stay together.
17. _____ Every society has a meaningful language.
18. _____ Adam had six sons whose descendants spread out across the world from Babel.
19. _____ Horticulturists grow cattle and other livestock.
20. _____ The source of all creation is God.

Complete these statements (each answer, 3 points).

21. Archaeologists are interested in man's _____ .
22. The mother of all people was _____ .
23. The bodies of all people are composed of common elements described in the Bible as _____ .
24. The three sons of Noah were Ham, Japheth, and _____ .
25. The Lord confused the language of people in the city of _____ .
26. Each parent contributes one *allele* for every _____ in a child.
27. The three races associated with the descendants of Noah are the Mongolid, Europid, and _____ .
28. An Eskimo house made of blocks of hard snow is called a(n) _____ .
29. According to the Bible (Genesis 1:27), "…God created man in His own _____ ."
30. A fieldworker in anthropology should keep a daily _____ .

Match these items (each answer, 2 points).

31. _____ list of marriages, births, deaths, and so forth
32. _____ reveals inner feelings
33. _____ began training ethnographers
34. _____ feast where wealth is given away
35. _____ group of related families
36. _____ having two feet; walking upright
37. _____ shock
38. _____ study every aspect of culture
39. _____ seeing primitive culture as superior to own
40. _____ digs up ancient ruins

a. Branislaw Malinowski
b. holistic
c. monograph
d. census
e. clan
f. trauma
g. psychological test
h. bipedal
i. potlatch
j. archaeologist
k. noble savage

64 / 80

Date _____

Score _____

1. c
2. b
3. a
4. d
5. c
6. c
7 a
8. b
9. a
10. d
11. false
12. false
13. true
14. true
15. false
16. true
17. true
18. false
19. false
20. true
21. past
22. Eve
23. dust
24. Shem
25. Babel
26. gene
27. Negrid
28. igloo
29. image
30. diary
31. d
32. g
33. a
34. i
35. e
36. h
37. f
38. b
39. k
40. j

Materials Needed for LIFEPAC

Required: Suggested:
None   atlas
                 encyclopedia

Additional Learning Activities

Section I An Introduction to Sociology

1. Discuss these questions with your class.
   a. How are sociology and psychology different? Who does the sociologist work with? Who does the psychologist work with? Invite a sociologist or a psychologist to visit the class and answer students' questions.
   b. Discuss a perfect society. How would a utopia differ from the society we have today? Can any society be completely perfect?
2. Describe to a friend your nuclear family. Then have your friend describe his extended family. Which turned out to be larger? Why?
3. Discuss socialization with your group. Why do some people grow up to be responsible, productive Christians and others to be criminals?
4. Write a brief report on propaganda and its uses. Is advertising a form of propaganda? Discuss this idea in your report.
5. What is a fad? Have you ever taken part in one? Are you still enthusiastic about it? What do sociologists say about fads?

Section II The Method of Sociology

1. Show the class some statistical charts or graphs and explain how they are used and what they mean. Have students ask as many questions as they can based on the charts and graphs.
2. If you can, obtain a copy of de Tocqueville's famous book *Democracy in America*, written in the last century, and read aloud certain brief passages of his observations on life in the United States. Are his observations still true today? Discuss why or why not.
3. Visit the home of a friend and write a brief case study of what you find there, as if you were a sociologist. If possible, have your friend return the visit and write a brief case study. Compare your case studies.
4. Think of three questions and conduct a random sampling of your class based on those questions. For example, you might ask each person his favorite sport. What conclusions can you draw from your survey?
5. Clip the results of a recent poll such as the Gallup Poll from the newspaper. What questions did it ask? How were the answers distributed? How would you have answered the questions?
6. Write a brief report on the lives of Durkheim, Weber, Sumner, or one of the other classical sociologists. How did he look at society? For what is he especially remembered?

SECTION ONE

1.1   b

1.2   d

1.3   f

1.4   h

1.5   g

1.6   e

1.7   c

1.8   a

1.9   true

1.10 true

1.11 false

1.12 true

1.13 true

1.14 false

1.15 true

1.16 true

1.17 **ACROSS**

1. diffusion
2. ethnocentrism
3. folkway
4. mores
5. positivism

DOWN

6. futurology
7. propaganda
8. socialization
9. utopia
10. epistemology

1.18 Groups are composed of individuals, which in turn, are influenced by the group.

1.19 Economics is the study of the production of goods and services.

1.20 Either order:
a. physical
b. cultural

1.21 Anthropology is the science that studies man.

1.22 c

1.23 e

1.24 f

1.25 d

1.26 a

1.27 b

1.28 social psychology

1.29 the origin and development of the different races of man.

1.30 b

1.31 a

1.32 c

1.33 d

1.34 d

1.35 a

1.36 b

1.37 Either order:
a. church
b. family

1.38 evolution

1.39 determinism

1.40 communism

1.41 A group is a set of people who are joined together by common interest.

1.42 a. institution
b. association
c. association
d. institution
e. association

1.43 a. S
b. P
c. P
d. P
e. S
f. S

1.44 Answers could include:
family—primary, church—primary, city—secondary

1.45 Culture is all the ways of thinking and acting that a person acquires from society.

1.46 It comes from our training as we grow up.

1.47 an Englishman

1.48 through language

1.49   Any order:
  a. gestures
  b. laughter
  c. songs
  d. military symbols
  e. bells
  f. processions
  g. crosses
  h. caps and gowns

1.50   Cultural accumulation is when one culture gradually takes on the culture of another society.

1.51   Cultural diffusion is the spread of traits from one culture to many other cultures.

1.52   Folkways

1.53   Mores

1.54   Ethnocentrism is when one culture is believed to be better than all others.

1.55   socialization

1.56   self-control

1.57   individual

1.58   Either order:
  a. emotional
  b. physical

1.59   life goals

1.60   self

1.61   loved

1.62   true

1.63   Either order:
  a. getting up in the morning
  b. delaying gratification

1.64   Any order:
  a. writing letters
  b. talking with new acquaintances
  c. using table manners

1.65   Collective behavior is behavior associated with relatively unorganized groups of people.

1.66   Examples:
  race riot, football game, fads

1.67   Emotional contagion is a shared or common emotional mood or experience.

1.68   A rumor is an unconfirmed or unfounded communication.

1.69   Public opinion is a shared opinion on some issue.

1.70   The aim of propaganda is to use the media to influence public opinion.

1.71   a. Christian groups are social.
  b. Christians can better understand their influence in a group.
  c. Christianity does affect culture.

1.72   a. where people live
  b. how many people move in or out of an area
  c. how many people die and are born in an area

SECTION TWO

2.1	e
2.2	a
2.3	c
2.4	f
2.5	d
2.6	b

2.7 a. society
     b. aspect
     c. pattern

2.8 suicide

2.9 static

2.10 false

2.11 Sociological description is the use of words to tell how something actually happened.

2.12 a. Alexis de Tocqueville
     b. *Democracy in America*

2.13 idealized

2.14 In the statistical approach, data is collected and used to test hypotheses.

2.15 A hypothesis is the possible answer or approach to a problem.

2.16 Probability is the possibility that something is true or valid.

2.17 Statistical analysis is called the historical method because collected data can be concerned with what has already occurred.

2.18 A sociological survey involves interviews to obtain relevant facts.

2.19 A selected sample is a representative group.

2.20 A random sample is something chosen by chance.

2.21 statistical
     description

2.22 b. small

2.23 a. an indication

2.24 Any order:
     a. by age
     b. by religion
     c. by education level
     d. by race
     e. by sex

2.25 Any order:
     a. description
     b. statistics
     c. survey
     d. experiment
     e. participant observation

2.26 Field

2.27 case

2.28 teacher check

SELF TEST 1

1.01 e
1.02 j
1.03 g
1.04 d
1.05 a
1.06 b
1.07 k
1.08 c
1.09 f
1.010 h
1.011 Either order:
    a. physical
    b. cultural
1.012 groups
1.013 kingdom
1.014 Either order:
    a. church
    b. family
1.015 institution
1.016 primary
1.017 family
1.018 secondary
1.019 culture

1.020 acquired
1.021 diffusion
1.022 individual
1.023 true
1.024 true
1.025 true
1.026 true
1.027 true
1.028 true
1.029 false
1.030 true
1.031 a. S
    b. P
    c. P
    d. P
    e. S
    f. S
1.032 Any order:
    a. population studies
    b. social groups
    c. cultural influences
    d. social changes
    e. social behavior

SELF TEST 2

2.01 c
2.02 e
2.03 a
2.04 g
2.05 f
2.06 d
2.07 b
2.08 b
2.09 a
2.010 d
2.011 b
2.012 c
2.013 hypothesis
2.014 theorists
2.015 society
2.016 description
2.017 *Democracy in America*

2.018 a. theories
    b. specific
2.019 research
2.020 a. data
    b. hypothesis
2.021 Probability
2.022 survey
2.023 sampling
2.024 random
2.025 Either order:
    a. family
    b. church
2.026 the family
2.027 A primary group is a close association of persons and is characterized by personal contact, mutual dependence and total involvement.

2.028 true
2.029 true
2.030 false
2.031 true

2.032 a. description
       b. statistics
       c. controlled experiments
       d. surveys
       e. field observation

History & Geography 705
LIFEPAC Test

1.	f	27.	false	
2.	a	28.	true	
3.	i	29.	false	
4.	k	30	group	
5.	e	31.	Philosophy	
6.	o	32.	diffusion	
7.	c	33.	culture	
8.	b	34.	probability	
9.	j	35.	Either order:	
10.	d		a. physical	
11.	g		b. cultural	
12.	h	36.	culture	
13.	m	37.	discipline	
14.	l	38.	emotional	
15.	true	39.	emotional	
16.	false	40	rumor	
17.	false	41.	government	
18.	true	42.	c	
19.	true	43.	a	
20.	true	44.	b	
21.	false	45.	b	
22.	true	46.	c	
23.	true	47.	a	
24.	true	48.	d	
25.	false	49.	b	
26.	true	50.	teacher check	

Name _____

Match these items (each answer, 2 points).

1. _____ sociology
2. _____ Marx and Engels
3. _____ probability
4. _____ utopia
5. _____ diffusion
6. _____ socialization
7. _____ propaganda
8. _____ group
9. _____ data
10. _____ institution

a. set of people with a common interest
b. ideal society
c. economic determinists
d. group that serves a public purpose
e. information
f. the study of society
g. influences public opinion
h. shared emotion
i. likelihood
j. spread of a cultural trait
k. makes an individual part of society

Answer *true* or *false* (each answer, 1 point).

11. _____ The nuclear family refers to father, mother, brothers, and sisters.
12. _____ Auguste Comte was the "father of sociology."
13. _____ Folkways are long-held customs.
14. _____ A fad is an example of collective behavior.
15. _____ Culture is hereditary.
16. _____ Herbert Spencer attempted to apply the theory of biological evolution to sociology.
17. _____ When a culture believes it is worse than all others, it is called ethnocentric.
18. _____ The most obvious example of a secondary group is the family.
19. _____ Sociology is concerned with individuals and not groups.
20. _____ The process through which an individual is made a part of society is called emotional contagion.

Complete these sentences (each answer, 3 points).

21. Emile Durkheim, the first scientific sociologist, was famous for his scientific study of _____ .
22. The Greek philosopher who imagined a completely planned, perfect society was _____ .
23. History is the study of man's _____ .
24. Random sampling is a general type of _____ .
25. A group in which members have close, personal contact is a _____ group.
26. Anthropology is the study of _____ .
27. A report made by a sociologist from field observations is called a(n) _____ .

28. In the Scripture the ideal society is the kingdom of _____ .
29. A shared opinion on a political or some other issue is called _____ opinion.
30. Futurology studies society's present and past to determine where it is headed in the _____ .

Write the letter for the correct answer on the line (each answer, 2 points).

31. The immediate family is the _____ family.
    a. extended   c. nuclear
    b. cultural   d. social
32. Grandparents, aunts, uncles, and cousins to which the nuclear family is related are the _____ family.
    a. extended   c. social
    b. cultural   d. primary
33. Sociology deals with _____ rather than individuals.
    a. pairs   c. families
    b. groups   d. utopias
34. The study of individual behavior is called _____ .
    a. economics   c. philosophy
    b. psychology   d. sociology
35. Plato's society was the first of many _____ .
    a. city-states   c. utopias
    b. republics   d. dictatorships
36. The basis for present-day communism was provided by _____ .
    a. Weber   c. Comte
    b. Durkheim   d. Marx
37. Asking people about themselves and their attitudes is known as a(n) _____ .
    a. survey   c. hypothesis
    b. quiz   d. data
38. Controlled experiments are used to give _____ of a group's reaction.
    a. an indication   c. a final conclusion
    b. a theory   d. a guess
39. Two kinds of anthropology are cultural and _____ .
    a. mathematical   c. biased
    b. psychological   d. physical
40. Culture is _____ , not inherited.
    a. collective   c. learned
    b. diffused   d. spoken

64 / 80

Date _____

Score _____

1. f
2. c
3. i
4. b
5. j
6. k
7. g
8. a
9. e
10. d
11. true
12. true
13. true
14. true
15. false
16. true
17. false
18. false
19. false
20. false
21. suicide
22. Plato
23. past
24. survey
25. primary
26. man
27. case study
28. God
29. public
30. future
31. c
32. a
33. b
34. b
35. c
36. d
37. a
38. a
39. d
40. c

Materials Needed for LIFEPAC

Required:
None

Suggested:
map of North America
encyclopedia

Additional Learning Activities

Section I Cultural Backgrounds of the States

1. Collect and display pictures of the various Native American cultures. Emphasize diversity of cultures and close relationship to natural environment.
2. Discuss false or prejudicial ideas about Native Americans and their way of life, such as "Eskimos live in igloos" or "Indians are better hunters."
3. Arrange for a class visit to a museum having Native American artifacts or to an Indian cultural center.
4. Dramatize a Northwest Indian potlatch after research into the customs, foods, and beliefs of these Indians. What types of gifts would be given away? What would the physical setting be like?
5. Select several native American tribes from different regions. Compare the ways in which they handled *one* of these phases of life:
   a. food-gathering and preservation
   b. personal adornment
   c. controlling bad behavior of tribal members
   d. caring for and educating children
   e. celebrations and recreation
   f. religious beliefs
   g. trade with other tribes. Make a written or oral report on your findings.
6. Report on one of the present-day controversies over Indian rights to land, fish, oil, irrigation water, police authority, or political power. What are possible solutions?

Section II Sociology and Culture of Groups from Distant Lands

1. Make sure students understand the immigration quota system, its rationale, present requirements, and control system. Discuss these quotas in light of current pressures such as illegal immigration from Mexico, refugees from Southeast Asia, and any local problems.
2. Discuss with the class examples of harmful stereotyping of national, racial, or occupational groups. Emphasize Christian responsibility in this area. Use local examples.
3. Have a naturalized citizen from another country speak to the class about his reasons for coming to America, experiences as an immigrant, and the process of becoming a citizen.

4. Tabulate the countries from which the ancestors of class members came to America. Plot these by pins placed on an outline map of the world. Remember that most people in America have several national ties, and that not everyone can be sure of their origins because family records are not complete.

5. If your community has any ethnic restaurants, obtain menus and find out about the ingredients of unfamiliar foods. If possible, make a class visit or have someone prepare one dish so that everyone can taste it.

6. Do a more thorough research study of one immigrant group, perhaps your own. Report to class.

7. The Statue of Liberty is the symbol of America's welcome to all peoples. Make a special report on its history and symbolism.

8. If your family has a special object, such as a picture, plate, basket, or piece of clothing brought to this country from their former home, ask if you may bring it to class. Remember that such items are irreplaceable and take good care of it.

9. The idea of social classes is often resisted by Americans. Discuss the social classes, their values, problems, and distinguishing characteristics. Emphasize that God does not consider social class important and that all classes share a common humanity.

Section III Cultural and Social Interaction

1. Discuss urbanization and its effects on American economic life, the family, and the church.

2. Using committees, prepare a group report on the changes in your own community in the past fifty years. Interview older people as well as using the library to collect information.

3. Debate the advantages of rural over city life or vice versa.

4. Collect and display photos with examples of body language. Try to use some from other cultures as well as our own.

5. Look at the list of cultural changes brought about by refrigeration on page 51 of the LIFEPAC. Develop a similar list based on another technological change, such as the telephone, central heating, or the CB radio, or computer.

6. Write a brief account of a tradition in your family, such as a special way of celebrating birthdays, a typical Thanksgiving, or an annual visit to a favorite vacation spot. Discuss with family members how this tradition was started.

ADDITIONAL ACTIVITY

This activity may be reproduced as a student worksheet.

| BELONGING | LOVE | SECURITY | ACHIEVEMENT |

| CHANGE | KNOWLEDGE | BEAUTY |

The boxes represent basic psychological needs. The following list names the experiences of a young child in a stable, loving family. Relate each experience to a need by writing the numbers below the correct boxes.

1. Says "Da-da," great family applause
2. Is taught to read at school
3. Eats at table with parents and grandparents
4. Falls down; is picked up and comforted
5. Bedroom is repainted
6. Father talks to and smiles at baby
7. Grandparents move away
8. Grandmother feeds and cuddles baby
9. Child arranges blocks in a straight row
10. Dog saves him in traffic
11. Is enrolled in Sunday school class
12. Learns songs, enjoys singing
13. Goes on long car trip with parents
14. Family has a new baby
15. Is allowed to go to neighborhood store alone for first time
16. Helps decorate Christmas cookies
17. Memorizes telephone number
18. Draws crayon pictures
19. Has regular mealtimes and bedtimes
20. Attends family reunion

SECTION ONE

1.1 **ACROSS**
1. adze
2. artifact
3. awl
4. breechcloth
5. emigrate
6. glacier
7. indigenous
8. leggings

DOWN
9. extinct
10. fowl
11. absolute
12. belief
13. custom

1.2 b
1.3 d
1.4 f
1.5 h
1.6 j
1.7 l
1.8 k
1.9 i
1.10 g
1.11 e
1.12 c
1.13 a
1.14 archaeologists
1.15 nomads
1.16 extinct
1.17 migrated
1.18 Bering Strait
1.19 c
1.20 e
1.21 g
1.22 a
1.23 h
1.24 f
1.25 d
1.26 b
1.27 Any order:
   a. Algonquian
   b. Iroquoian

1.28 Any order:
   a. bone
   b. stone
   c. wood
1.29 a. W
   b. B
   c. W
   d. L
   e. L
1.30 b
1.31 Any order:
   a. squash
   b. beans
   c. pumpkin
   d. corn
   e. tobacco
1.32 wampum
1.33 a. League
   b. Hiawatha
1.34 Confederacy
1.35 c
1.36 b
1.37 Any order:
   a. Cayuga
   b. Mohawk
   c. Oneida
   d. Onondaga
   e. Seneca
1.38 Tuscaroras
1.39 a. Natchez
   b. Mobiles
   c. Wacos
   d. Creeks
1.40 Cahokia
1.41 a. fruit
   b. baskets
   c. pearls
1.42 salt
1.43 Cherokee
1.44 diseases
1.45 false
1.46 true
1.47 true

1.48 false
1.49 true
1.50 false
1.51 true
1.52 false
1.53 pueblos
1.54 a. _X_
b. __
c. _X_
d. _X_
e. __
f. __
g. _X_
h. _X_
1.55 a. __
b. _X_
c. _X_
d. _X_
e. _X_
f. _X_
g. __
1.56 a. _X_
b. __
c. _X_
d. __
e. _X_
1.57 a. __
b. _X_
c. __
d. _X_
e. _X_
f. __
g. __
1.58 a. _X_
b. __
c. _X_
d. __
e. __
f. __
g. _X_
h. _X_
i. _X_
j. _X_
1.59 lamps
1.60 raw meat

1.61 a. _X_
b. _X_
c. __
d. __
e. __
f. _X_
g. _X_
h. __
1.62 Either order:
a. Marquesas Islands
b. Tahiti
1.63 a. M
b. C
c. W
d. M
e. W
f. W
1.64 a. _X_
b. __
c. _X_
d. __
e. _X_
f. __
g. _X_
h. _X_
i. _X_
j. __
1.65 king
1.66 teacher check

SECTION TWO

2.1	c
2.2	e
2.3	g
2.4	i
2.5	a
2.6	h
2.7	f
2.8	d
2.9	b
2.10	immigrants
2.11	Anglo-Saxons
2.12	Germans
2.13	Pennsylvania Dutch
2.14	Italians
2.15	true
2.16	true
2.17	false
2.18	true
2.19	true
2.20	g
2.21	d
2.22	i
2.23	a
2.24	h
2.25	b
2.26	k
2.27	c
2.28	f
2.29	l
2.30	Hawaii
2.31	Gold Hill
2.32	false
2.33	false
2.34	true
2.35	true
2.36	true
2.37	true
2.38	teacher check
2.39	c
2.40	e
2.41	b
2.42	f
2.43	d
2.44	a
2.45	true

2.46	true
2.47	false
2.48	true
2.49	true
2.50	true
2.51	Any order:
	a. Buddhism
	b. Hinduism
	c. Islam
	d. Christianity
	e. Judaism
2.52	one-sixth
2.53	ghettos
2.54	Any order:
	a. upper
	b. middle
	c. poor
	or lower
2.55	Any order:
	a. money
	b. occupation
	c. education

SECTION THREE

3.1   a. ___
      b. ___
      c. ✓
      d. ___
      e. ___
      f. ✓

3.2   c

3.3   d

3.4   a

3.5   b

3.6   technology

3.7   machines

3.8   industrialized

3.9   false

3.10 Any order:
      a. family
      b. education
      c. religion
      d. government
      e. economic

3.11 Stable

3.12 school

3.13 industrialization

3.14 assimilation

3.15 true

3.16 false

3.17 true

3.18 true

3.19 true

3.20 jobs

3.21 urbanization

3.22 values

3.23 roles

3.24 isolated

3.25 class

3.26 Either order:
      a. Poor people are left in central cities.
      b. More cars are needed.

3.27 older

3.28 Any order:
      a. Who will earn the money?
      b. Who will cook the food?
      c. Adults have less time for each other.

SELF TEST 1

1.01	b	1.020	b
1.02	d	1.021	a
1.03	f	1.022	a
1.04	g	1.023	b
1.05	a	1.024	a
1.06	e	1.025	c
1.07	c	1.026	c
1.08	true	1.027	b
1.09	false	1.028	d
1.010	false	1.029	a
1.011	true	1.030	c
1.012	false	1.031	c
1.013	false	1.032	b
1.014	false	1.033	buffalo
1.015	false	1.034	Hawaii
1.016	false	1.035	Spanish
1.017	true	1.036	potlatch
1.018	c	1.037	Bering Strait
1.019	c	1.038	raw meat

SELF TEST 2

2.01	true	2.022	h
2.02	false	2.023	j
2.03	true	2.024	g
2.04	false	2.025	k
2.05	false	2.026	i
2.06	false	2.027	c
2.07	true	2.028	e
2.08	true	2.029	a
2.09	false	2.030	f
2.010	f	2.031	Any order:
2.011	a		a. Sweden
2.012	e		b. Finland
2.013	d		c. Norway
2.014	c		d. Denmark
2.015	c	2.032	Japanese
2.016	a	2.033	Russians
2.017	a	2.034	Any order:
2.018	b		a. Cuba
2.019	c		b. Puerto Rico
2.020	c		c. Mexico
2.021	d	2.035	Louisiana

2.036	b	2.039	a
2.037	d	2.040	e
2.038	f	2.041	c

SELF TEST 3

3.01	false	3.021		diseases
3.02	true	3.022	a.	homes
3.03	true		b.	shops
3.04	false	3.023	a.	Asia
3.05	true		b.	Bering Strait
3.06	false	3.024		Any order:
3.07	false		a.	money
3.08	true		b.	education
3.09	a		c.	occupation
3.010	b	3.025		buffalo
3.011	d	3.026		English
3.012	c	3.027		industrialized
3.013	c	3.028		Any order:
3.014	b		a.	Buddhism
3.015	c		b.	Hinduism
3.016	d		c.	Islam
3.017	b		d.	Judaism
3.018	a		e.	Christianity
3.019	Any order:	3.029		assimilation
	a. economic	3.030		bilingual
	b. government	3.031		technology
	c. religion	3.032		urbanization
3.020	Irish			

History & Geography 706
LIFEPAC Test

1. true
2. false
3. true
4. false
5. true
6. true
7. true
8. false
9. true
10. false
11. dialect
12. Any order:
    a. English
    b. Scotch
    c. Welsh
13. a. pierced
    b. tattooed
14. b
15. c
16. a
17. language
18. Any two:
    a. Chinese
    b. Japanese
       or Native American, Russians

19. melting pot
20. Cherokee
21. Any order:
    a. upper
    b. middle
    c. poor
       or lower
22. c
23. g
24. h
25. e
26. a
27. j
28. f
29. d
30. k
31. b
32. d
33. d
34. c
35. a
36. c
37. b
38. a
39. d

Name _____

Answer *true* or *false* (each answer, 1 point).

1. _____ People can be grouped by age, national origin, geography, and in many other ways.
2. _____ The early inhabitants of the Hawaiian Islands were Polynesians who came from the Marquesas, another island group.
3. _____ People from England, Scotland, and Wales were the first major group of white settlers along the Atlantic seaboard.
4. _____ Very few immigrants came to America from Italy.
5. _____ American Indians believed land was to be used well, but not owned.
6. _____ Eskimos used only the best meat from seals and whales and discarded the rest of the carcasses.
7. _____ The most important game animal for the Plains Indians was the moose.
8. _____ Potlatch celebrations were part of the culture of the Northwest Coast Indians.
9. _____ The early nomads who settled North America probably came across the Bering Strait to what is now Alaska.
10. _____ Many immigrant groups were subjected to prejudice and discrimination in this country.

Complete these statements (each answer, 3 points).

11. Three basic psychological needs of all people are a. _____, b. _____, and c. _____.
12. Three important educational institutions are the a. _____, b. _____, and c. _____.
13. Three holidays celebrated *only* in the United States are a. _____, b. _____, and c. _____.
14. Urbanization means _____ _____.
15. Because the United States has absorbed people, customs, and languages from many countries and cultures, we call it a _____ pot.
16. Three tribes of American Indians that live in the Southwest are the a. _____, b. _____, and c. _____.
17. Three famous American Indian leaders were a. _____, b. _____, and c. _____.
18. Social class in America is determined largely by a. _____, b. _____, and c. _____.
19. Three basic institutions in all societies are a. _____, b. _____, and c. _____.
20. When religion is a dominant force in a person's life, it gives the individual a. _____, b. _____, and c. _____.

Match these items (each answer, 2 points).

21. _____	Mormons	a. the merging of elements from two or more cultures into one
22. _____	body language	
23. _____	Sequoyah	b. black explorer of the Southwest
24. _____	ethnic	c. able to speak two languages
25. _____	Japanese	d. invented a written Cherokee language
26. _____	assimilation	e. facial expressions, postures, or movements which convey meaning
27. _____	Estevanico	
28. _____	travois	f. religious group that settled in Utah
29. _____	artifact	g. device made of poles for dragging supplies
30. _____	bilingual	h. based on nationality or race
		i. physical remains of a culture, such as tools.
		j. one of the groups of immigrants from Asia
		k. masks worn by Indian dancers

Write the letter for the correct answer on each line (each answer, 2 points).

31. American society, composed of many different national groups, is a _____ society.
    a. monopolistic
    b. chauvinistic
    c. pluralistic
    d. communistic

32. Eskimo survival was based on _____ .
    a. inherited wealth
    b. hunting and fishing
    c. agriculture
    d. trade with many other groups

33. The institution in society that satisfies most of the individual's psychological needs is the _____ .
    a. government
    b. neighborhood
    c. family
    d. school

34. An example of technological change that has deeply affected society is _____ .
    a. the automobile
    b. television
    c. rainfall
    d. both a and b

35. Rural life usually provides more _____ than city life does.
    a. employment
    b. commercial entertainment
    c. class distinction
    d. interpersonal relationships

36. When they encountered the native American cultures, the white men _____ .
    a. assimilated many useful things
    b. went back to Europe
    c. established no contacts
    d. changed completely to native American ways

37. Mardi Gras is a holiday based on _____ .
    a. the Buddhist religion
    b. the Jewish religion
    c. Christian tradition
    d. French independence celebration

38. Black people have not kept up strong connections with their original cultures in Africa because _____ .
    a. they came too late
    b. slavery prevented communication and broke up many black families
    c. they preferred American ways
    d. they tried to forget their old ways

99 / 124

Date _____

Score _____

1. true
2. true
3. true
4. false
5. true
6. false
7. false
8. true
9. true
10. true
11. Examples; any order:
    a. love
    b. belonging
    c. sense of achievement, beauty, or fulfillment
12. Any order:
    a. home
    b. school
    c. church
13. Any three:
    a. Martin Luther King's birthday
    b. Lincoln's birthday
    c. Washington's birthday or Groundhog Day, Arbor Day Pulaski's birthday Mother's Day Father's Day Memorial Day Flag Day Independent Day Labor Day Columbus Day
14. an increase in city living
15. melting
16. Any three:
    a. Hopi
    b. Navajo
    c. Apache or Zuni, Pima, or Papago

17. Any three:
    a. Geronimo
    b. Cochise
    c. Crazy Horse
18. Any order:
    a. money
    b. occupation
    c. education
19. Examples; any order:
    a. family
    b. schools
    c. churches or businesses
20. Any three:
    a. strength
    b. direction
    c. faith or support, or peace of mind
21. f
22. e
23. d
24. h
25. j
26. a
27. b
28. g
29. i
30. c
31. c
32. b
33. c
34. d
35. d
36. a
37. c
38. b

Materials Needed for LIFEPAC

Required:

Suggested:
wall map of the world,
wall map of the Middle East showing ancient countries, cities, and
topography of Abraham's time

Additional Learning Activities

Section I   The Earth Is Man's Home

1. Discuss with students the responsibility in stewardship that man has toward God if one believes that God is the owner of all creation.
2. Discuss with students the three races of man that came forth from Noah's three sons.
3. Discuss with students in what way Noah was like a modern day zookeeper.
4. Discuss with students the dividing line between prehistory and history.
5. Take a trip to a museum where you can see items of prehistoric interest.
6. Conduct a Bible search on longevity. Find the genealogies located in Genesis 5. Then find out the ages of the following people to see how long early man lived—Adam, Seth, Enos, Canaan, Mahalaleel, Jared, Enoch, Methuselah, Lamech. In addition, list the things that man had learned to do before the Flood.
7. Look up the five steps in the scientific method. Write a report or give an oral report in which you discuss evolution in relation to the steps of the scientific method.

Section II   The Earth Is Developed by Man

1. Discuss with students the areas of the world where great population densities exist. Discuss with students the advantages as well as the problems associated with great population density.
2. Discuss with students why civilizations developed in particular areas of the world. What factors contributed to the development?
3. Discuss with students the importance of navigation in modern society.
4. Invite an environmental expert or a geologist to speak to the class on natural resources, their importance in our lives and what can occur as their supplies are depleted.
5. Visit a museum that features early navigational equipment or visit a museum that features early industrial equipment.
6. Visit a factory for a tour. When you return, discuss the adaptation of older methods of mass production you saw in your visit to the modern factory.

7. Interview an elderly citizen in your community. Ask him questions, such as, "Did you grow up in a rural or urban area?" How many times and how far have you moved during your lifetime?" "What forms of transportation were common when you were young?" "How has industry changed during your lifetime." "What kind of work did you do during your lifetime?"How much education was normal when you were of school age?" Make a report to the rest of the class.

8. Research a problem that is directly related to the Industrial Revolution. Write a report on that problem and give suggestions for its solution.

Section III The Earth Has a Future

1. Discuss with students the effect governmental controls have on the liberties Christians desire to propagate the Gospel of Jesus Christ.

2. Discuss with students the effects of war on individual lives. Invite a theologian to your class to discuss in more detail God's plan for man's eternal habitat.

3. Have a group discussion on the ways Christians may lead a Godlike life in the face of world evils and in preparation for Christ's judgment.

4. Keep a current affairs notebook. Include in your notebook items from newspapers that indicate the end time is near.

5. Interview a visiting missionary to determine if the Gospel is being preached among all nations. Prepare a report to the class on the subject.

SECTION ONE

1.1	one large continent
1.2	Arizona
1.3	c
1.4	b
1.5	c
1.6	b
1.7	a
1.8	d
1.9	c
1.10	c
1.11	d
1.12	b
1.13	c
1.14	a
1.15	a
1.16	b
1.17	Fertile Crescent
1.18	Babel
1.19	language
1.20	confounded
1.21	Sumerians
1.22	Babylon
1.23	Ur
1.24	1400 B.C.
1.25	Any order:
	a. Japheth; Europe
	b. Ham; Africa
	c. Shem; China

1.26	true
1.27	true
1.28	true
1.29	false
1.30	true
1.31	true
1.32	Either order:
	a. Kish
	b. Nippur
1.33	Hammurabi
1.34	Hittites
1.35	Menes
1.36	Pharaohs
1.37	Memphis
1.38	hieroglyphics
1.39	Phoenicians
1.40	famine
1.41	Either order:
	a. Hebrew
	b. Arabic
1.42	teacher check

SECTION TWO

2.1	c
2.2	e
2.3	d
2.4	e
2.5	b
2.6	c
2.7	f
2.8	a
2.9	a
2.10	e
2.11	d
2.12	f
2.13	g or h

2.14	h
2.15	g or h
2.16	h
2.17	h
2.18	c
2.19	Mediterranean
2.20	Minoan
2.21	Either order:
	a. plumbing
	b. paintings
2.22	Mycenaean
2.23	a. Egyptians
	b. Phoenicians

2.24 Either order:
    a. history
    b. science
2.25 400s B.C.
2.26 Any order:
    a. Etruscans
    b. Greeks
    c. Egyptians
2.27 Any order:
    a. roads
    b. aqueducts
    c. coded laws
    or Latin
2.28 d
2.29 c
2.30 a
2.31 d
2.32 b
2.33 a
2.34 b
2.35 b
2.36 b
2.37 Any order:
    a. Ethiopia
    b. Bantus
    c. Hottentots
    d. Nubians
    e. Kongo
      or Lubas, Aksum, Ghana, Mali
2.38 Either order:
    a. They intermarried with them.
    b. They pushed them into the rain
       forest or desert to live.
2.39 a
2.40 b
2.41 c
2.42 c
2.43 a
2.44 b
2.45 b
2.46 a
2.47 c
2.48 false
2.49 true
2.50 true

2.51 true
2.52 false
2.53 true
2.54 Either order:
    a. Tyre
    b. Sidon
2.55 Either order:
    a. Carthaginians
    b. Greeks
2.56 compass
2.57 Leif Erickson
2.58 Robert Fulton
2.59 canals
2.60 Either order:
    a. Panama
    b. Suez
2.61 dredging
2.62 Either order:
    a. diesel
    b. nuclear (atomic)
2.63 Either order:
    a. oars
    b. sails
2.64 b
2.65 d
2.66 a
2.67 a
2.68 c
2.69 b
2.70 d
2.71 Example:
Open-pit mines could be filled and
covered once mining is completed.
The ground could be brought back to
its original contours and planted with
grass, trees, or crops.
2.72 a
2.73 c
2.74 b
2.75 Any order:
    a. availability of jobs
    b. access to religious and cultural
       activities
    c. breakdown of feudal system or
       looking for better way of life

2.76 Any order:
   a. United States
   b. Canada
   c. India

2.77 Any order:
   a. railroads
   b. canals
   c. by sea or by turnpike

2.78 Either order:
   a. dams
   b. aqueducts
   or irrigation

2.79 teacher check

2.80 Either order:
   a. coal
   b. petroleum

2.81 sludge

2.82 Example:
the study of living organisms in relationship to their environment

2.83 Example:
dumping pollutants into the air and water to be carried away

2.84 Example:
It would mean the recycling of natural resources that would otherwise be wasted. Scarring of the land could be repaired. Water and air would not be poisoned as they are now.

SECTION THREE

3.1 b

3.2 a

3.3 c

3.4 c

3.5 Examples:
   a. Diplomacy is the art and practice of conducting negotiations between nations.
   b. Nations desiring to live in peace should use diplomacy in a spirit of tolerance and understanding of the point of view of others.

3.6 Example:
The Antichrist will likely be a proud, vain deceiver. He will cause all men to live under his bondage to satisfy his greed for power. He will sacrifice any-one who stands in his way.

3.7 lamb

3.8 Jerusalem

3.9 rearranged

3.10 Either order:
   a. heavens
   b. firmament

3.11 Daniel

3.12 judge

3.13 peace

3.14 thousand

3.15 saints

3.16 God in heaven

3.17 Example:
They shall not eat meat; "the lion shall eat straw like the ox."

3.18 Any order:
   a. tears
   b. death
   c. sorrow
   d. crying
   e. pain

SELF TEST 1

1.01	5		1.026	the sun's radiation
1.02	8		1.027	strata
1.03	3		1.028	petroleum
1.04	1		1.029	g
1.05	9		1.030	h
1.06	10		1.031	e
1.07	4		1.032	c
1.08	6		1.033	b
1.09	7		1.034	a
1.010	2		1.035	i
1.011	c		1.036	j
1.012	i		1.037	f
1.013	j		1.038	d
1.014	a		1.039	l

1.015 b
1.016 l
1.017 h
1.018 e
1.019 d
1.020 f
1.021 k
1.022 Mesopotamia
1.023 Sumerians
1.024 Adam
1.025 God

1.040–1.042   Examples:
1.040   Oil and coal were formed from dead animals and plants over a period of years.
1.041   The land was everywhere the same; the climate was like a hothouse: warm and humid. The soil was rich.
1.042   Mountain ranges and volcanoes appeared; chasms opened. Hills fell. Oceans washed beaches away.

SELF TEST 2

2.01	b		2.017	b
2.02	a		2.018	j
2.03	c		2.019	d
2.04	b		2.020	e
2.05	a		2.021	Either order:
2.06	c			a. coal
2.07	b			b. petroleum
2.08	c		2.022	nuclear
2.09	a		2.023	fossil
2 010	a		2.024	replenish or subdue
2.011	g		2.025	a. Ararat
2.012	k			b. Turkey
2.013	a		2.026	Lydians
2.014	i		2.027	Assyrians
2.015	f		2.028	Hebrew
2.016	c		2.029	Chinese

2.030	Mayans	2.035	true
2.031	a. Andes	2.036	true
	b. South America	2.037	true
2.032	Aztec	2.038	c
2.033	Either order:	2.039	d
	a. compass	2.040	e
	b. astrolabe	2.041	a
2.034	Either order:	2.042	b
	a. Panama		
	b. Suez		

SELF TEST 3

3.01	false	3.027	a
3.02	true	3.028	h
3.03	true	3.029	f
3.04	false	3.030	a
3.05	false	3.031	f
3.06	false	3.032	e
3.07	true	3.033	e
3.08	true	3.034	g
3.09	false	3.035	e
3.010	true	3.036	d
3.011	England	3.037	a
3.012	Babel	3.038	c
3.013	glacier		

3.014 Either order:
a. Panama
b. Suez
3.015 open-pit
3.016 the flood
3.017 Armageddon
3.018 Antichrist
3.019 ten
3.020 League of Nations
3.021 Either order:
a. coal
b. petroleum
3.022 Middle East
3.023 conquering lamb
3.024 b
3.025 g
3.026 c

3.039–3041 Examples:
3.039 Oil and coal were formed from dead animals and plants under the pressure of tons of rocks and mud over thousands of years.
3.040 The topography will be rearranged. Mountains and islands will be moved. Stars will fall into the oceans, killing marine life. Rivers will be poisoned.
3.041 Men will be with God and He with them. There will be no more tears, death, sorrow, crying or pain. Everything will be new.

History & Geography 906
LIFEPAC Test

1. b

2. c

3. a

4. c

5. a

6. b

7. d

8. a

9. b

10. c

11. Example:
They used water craft or simple and primitive construction.

12. Example:
Ecology is the study of living organisms in relationship to their environment.

13. Example:
reusing refuse such as metal, glass, and paper to make new products

14. h

15. c

16. d

17. a

18. g

19. f

20. i

21. e

22. j

23. b

24. 2

25. 3

26. 5

27. 4

28. 1

29. 7

30. 6

31. Examples:
   a. using sludge for fertilizer
   b. using sewage for landfill
   c. recycling glass and paper

32. Any order:
   a. no more tears
   b. no more death
   c. no more sorrow
   d. no more pain
   e. no more crying

33. Antichrist

34. one

35. League of Nations

36. conquering lamb

37. rearranged

38. d

39. a

40. e

41. b

42. c

Name _____

Write the letter for the correct answer on each line (each answer, 2 points).

1.   The earth's first climate _____ .
        a. was very cold   c. was spring-like
        b. was harsh   d. had four seasons

2.   The confusion of man's languages happened at _____ .
        a. Babel   c. Phoenicia
        b. Memphis   d. Kish

3.   The Sumerians used wedge-shaped characters in their alphabet for writing
        in clay. This type of writing was called _____ .
        a. cuneiform   c. papyrus
        b. hieroglyphic   d. lettering

4.   Before sinning, early man lived _____ .
        a. a long life span   c. in the trees
        b. in fear of dinosaurs   d. as a protoman

5.   A blend of two metals is known as _____ .
        a. open pit mining   c. ductile
        b. an outflow   d. an alloy

6.   Mining was revived after the _____ .
        a. Dark Ages passed   c. tower of Babel fell
        b. atomic age arrived   d. Golden Age came

7.   During the Industrial Revolution many cities in Europe were _____ .
        a. very dirty and crowded c. abandoned
        b. like paradise   d. paved

8.   Merchants from Europe expanded trade in the new world by selling their
        wares in _____ .
        a. the Orient   c. their colonies in America
        b. India   d. Siberia

9.   The waste that causes a buildup of sludge in river bottoms is called

        _____ .

        a. slag   c. smog
        b. effluent   d. alloy

10.   The greatest source of air pollution is from _____ .
        a. generating electricity from coal
        b. hydroelectric generation of electricity
        c. dumping garbage at city dumps

Complete these activities (each answer, 5 points).

11.   How did man develop nature's resources to provide for his city's water supply? _____

_____

_____

12.   How did man develop nature's resources to provide for his city's energy needs? _____

_____

_____

13.   How did man develop nature's resources to provide for his city's transportation needs? _____

_____

_____

Match these items (each answer, 2 points).

14.   _____ pestilence
15.   _____ deluge
16.   _____ millennium
17.   _____ ecology
18.   _____ refinery
19.   _____ famine
20.   _____ technology
21.   _____ antichrist
22.   _____ clipper
23.   _____ marsh

a. Noah's Flood
b. a drought
c. raw materials become merchandise
d. a plague of insects
e. a sailing ship
f. one thousand years
g. development of better engineering skills
h. a swampy area
i. mark of the beast
j. a good balance in nature

Complete these statements (each answer, 3 points).

24. The metal that is more ductile than other metals is _____ .
25. Dirty air is called _____ .
26. The Mediterranean is the name of a _____ .
27. Rome is a great city in the country of _____ .
28. Armaggedon will be a place of _____ .
29. The wicked shall be judged and sent to _____ .
30. The present earth will be destroyed by _____ .
31. The city that will come down out of heaven will be _____ .
32. The ruler during the millennium will be _____ .
33. Those who study the earth's topography are called _____ .

Write the letter for the correct answer on the line (each answer, 2 points).

34. Jesus Christ is called _____ .
    a. the king of Babylon
    b. a warmonger
    c. the Prince of Peace
35. Charles Darwin was _____ .
    a. a Creationist
    b. an evolutionist
    c. a prophet
36. Daniel Jackling advanced the idea of _____ .
    a. open pit mining
    b. the theory of evolution
    c. city planning
37. Around A.D. 1000 the Vikings were great explorers.
    They were from _____ .
    a. Norway and Denmark
    b. Russia
    c. Phoenicia
38. The people who established city-states along the Tigris and Euphrates rivers
    were the _____ .
    a. Greeks
    b. Egyptians
    c. Sumerians

Date _____

Score _____

1. c
2. a
3. a
4. a
5. d
6. a
7. a
8. c
9. b
10. a
11. He dammed up rivers and created reservoirs to hold lakes of water. Then he built water filtering systems to clean up his water so that he could drink it. In some places he used canals to irrigate farms near his cities.

12. He built hydroelectric plants in the dams he built on rivers. He also built coal and oil-burning generators so that electricity could be provided for the cities.

13. He built modern highways, streets and freeways as well as subways and railways to transport the people to and around in his cities.
14. d
15. a
16. f
17. j
18. c
19. b
20. g
21. i
22. e
23. h
24. gold

25. smog
26. sea
27. Italy
28. war, battle
29. hell
30. fire
31. New Jerusalem
32. Jesus Christ
33. geologists
34. c
35. b
36. a
37. a
38. c